S0-BBB-048

PORCHES

PORCHES

BARRON'S

Introduction

The Idea of the Porch

Veranda, piazza, gallery, portico, stoop, loggia, colonnade, corredor, galerie…these are all words that have become synonymous with the term "porch." But that's not to say that these words all describe the same thing, because they don't; they describe distinctively different architectural features. There is one thing they all have in common, however—*the idea of the porch*. It was this concept that President George Bush (Sr.) evoked in his inaugural address in 1989:

"We meet on democracy's front porch, a good place to talk as friends. For this is a day when our nation is made whole, when our differences, for a moment, are suspended."

The word "porch" comes from the Latin *porticus*. It is related to both "portal" and "passage." Within the word origins are suggestions of *transportation* or at least *movement*—the porch being something through which one must pass. And while the most common image of the American porch consists of a

relaxing oasis troubled only by the gentle motion of a rocking chair, there is also the fact that it connects *in* with *out*. The porch plays an active as well as a passive role.

The porch also conveys a notion of neighborliness and openness to the world. There is something so inviting about it, which is why it's such a "good place to talk as friends."

And the idea of the porch being a place where "all differences are suspended" includes in it all the synonyms mentioned at the start and the worlds they represent—the Spanish, the French, the Dutch, the urban, the Midwestern, the blue collar and the gubernatorial. From the inner-city stoop to the Louisiana veranda, the porch has become a symbolic place in the American mind—a *feeling*, if you will, as comforting to the romantic teenager as to the quilt-wrapped elder.

Throughout the following pages, we have tried to capture the true essence of the porch in its many forms, both through photographs and familiar literary quotations. So pull up a rocking chair and enjoy!

With its numerous associations, the porch awakens something deep in American consciousness. It is a reminder of America's past. Its appearance coincided with the founding of the nation.

The porch is a populist symbol par excellence. Time has made of it a symbol for the individual's ties to the family and, by extension, to the nation as an enlargement of the family. The porch is where friends meet to share a few quiet words, a place of reflection where old folk sit and watch the world go by, where teenagers take their first hesitant steps in romantic love, where grief spends itself, and hope blossoms. The American porch is a bridge to the universe.

Philip Drew
Veranda: Embracing Place

In this country, no architectural feature is more plainly expressive of purpose in our dwelling-houses than the *veranda*, or piazza. The unclouded splendor and fierce heat of our summer sun, render this very general appendage a source of real comfort and enjoyment; and the long veranda round many of our country residences stand in stead of the paved terraces of the English mansions as the place for promenade; while during the warmer portions of the season, half of the days or evenings are there passed in the enjoyment of the cool breezes, secure under low roofs supported by the open colonnade, from the solar rays, or the dews of night. The obvious utility of the veranda in this climate, (especially in the middle and southern states,) will, therefore, excuse its adoption into any style of architecture that may be selected for our domestic uses, although abroad, buildings in the style in question, as the Gothic, for example, are not usually accompanied by such an appendage. An artist of the least taste or invention, will easily compose an addition, of this kind, that will be in good keeping with the rest of the edifice.

Andrew Jackson Downing
Landscape Architecture

They topped the rise and the white house reared its perfect symmetry before her, tall of columns, wide of verandas, flat of roof, beautiful as a woman who is so sure of her charm that she can be generous and gracious to all.

Margaret Mitchell
Gone With The Wind

...And it has become that time of evening when people sit on their porches, rocking gently and talking gently and watching the street and the standing up into their sphere of possession of the trees, of birds hung havens, hangars. People go by; things go by. A horse, drawing a buggy, breaking his hollow iron music on the asphalt; a loud auto; a quiet auto; people in pairs, not in a hurry, scuffling, switching their weight of aestival body, talking casually, the taste hovering over them of vanilla, strawberry, pasteboard and starched milk, the image upon them of lovers and horsemen, squared with clowns in hueless amber.

James Agee
A Death in the Family

Across the street and down the way the other houses stood with their flat fronts. What was it Clarise had said one afternoon? "No front porches. My uncle says there used to be front porches. And people sat there sometimes at night, talking when they wanted to talk, rocking, and not talking when they didn't want to talk. Sometimes they just sat there and thought about things, turned things over. My uncle says the architects got rid of the porches because they didn't look well. But my uncle says that was merely rationalising it; the real reason, hidden underneath, might be they didn't like people sitting like that, doing nothing, rocking, talking; that was the wrong kind of social life."

Ray Bradbury
Fahrenheit 451

Generations of listeners on front porches in Selma have grown up hearing about how a bank president hid gold inside the tall columns in his home when the Yankees invaded Selma. The column with a plugged hole at the top where he dropped the gold in and a plugged hole at the bottom where he later took it out is still there at the Quarles home on Lapsley Street.

Kathryn Tucker Windham
Alabama: One Big Front Porch

The Radley Place jutted into a sharp
curve beyond our house. Walking
south, one faced its porch; the sidewalk
turned and ran beside the lot. The house
was low, was once white with a deep front
porch and green shutters, but had long
ago darkened to the color of the slate-grey
yard around it. Rain-rotten shingles
drooped over the eaves of the veranda;
oak trees kept the sun away. The remains
of a picket drunkenly guarded the front
yard—a "swept" yard that was never
swept—where johnson grass and rabbit-
tobacco grew in abundance.

Harper Lee
To Kill A Mockingbird

Eliza stood upon the porch, her hands clasped loosely across her stomach. Eugene was leaving the house and going toward the town. It was the day before his departure; dusk was coming on, the hills were blooming in strange purple dusk. Eliza watched him go.

"Spruce up there, boy!" she called. "Spruce up! Throw your shoulders back!"

Thomas Wolfe
Look Homeward, Angel

Note in passing the architectural side effect of the fresh-air cult, as the houses of the prosperous and the apartment buildings multiplying for them in larger cities west of Pittsburgh sprouted screened sleeping porches—sensible for summer but also doughtily used in winter by many families able to persuade themselves that natural refrigeration was just what they and their children needed.

J. C. Furnas
The Americans: A Social History Of the United States 1587–1914

S lenderly, languidly, their hands set lightly on their hips, the two young women preceded us out onto a rosy-colored porch, open toward the sunset, where four candles flickered on the table in the diminished wind.

"Why candles?" objected Daisy, frowning. She snapped them out with her fingers. "In two weeks it'll be the longest day in the year." She looked at us all radiantly. "Do you always watch for the longest day of the year and then miss it? I always watch for the longest day of the year and then miss it."

F. Scott Fitzgerald
The Great Gatsby

Mary Aston did not see Edward and his sister, as she was intent upon training up a honey-suckle to one of the carved urns pendant from the projection of the house. Edward stopped to watch for a moment her delicate white fingers as they moved among the leaves and flowers. Her mother was sitting in the porch, with her eyes fixed upon the shaggy house dog, which was once her husband's. The dog was lying upon the step, with his neck stretched out over the door-sill, and resting partly on his mistress' feet. He was the first to notice the visitors. He turned round his head, got up and shook himself very deliberately, and then looked up in his mistress' face, as if asking how he was to receive the new comers.

Richard Henry Dana Sr.
From "Edward and Mary"

The screen door slams,
    Mary's dress waves.
Like a vision she dances across the porch
As the radio plays
Roy Orbison singing for the lonely
Hey that's me and I want you only
Don't turn me home again
I just can't face myself alone again.

Bruce Springsteen
From "Thunder Road"

The porch is the soul of a house. Poor and spiritless indeed is that structure which lacks it....Imagine going right into a house, with no gracious lingering on a porch! Or of stepping out of the door to find oneself on the alien pavement! Such procedure outrages all the amenities of life. True gentility is inseparable from a porch. Somewhere in the past of every courtly soul will be found a benignant porch, stretching its influence over the years.

Dorothy Scarborough
From A Southern Porch

You could not put your finger on it, but you knew these women shared secret lagoons of knowledge. Secret codes and lore and lingo stretching back into that fluid time before air conditioning dried up the rich, heavy humidity that used to hang over the porches of Louisiana, drenching cotton blouses, beads of sweat tickling the skin, slowing people down so the world entered them in an unhurried way. A thick stew of life that seeped into the very blood of people, so that eccentric, languid thoughts simmered inside.

Rebecca Wells
Divine Secrets of the Ya-Ya Sisterhood

The path to Bunbury seemed little traveled, but it was distinct enough and ran through the trees in a zigzag course until it finally led them to an open space filled with the queerest houses Dorothy had ever seen. They were all made of crackers, laid out in tiny squares, and were of many pretty and ornamental shapes, having balconies and porches with posts of bread-sticks and roofs shingled with wafer-crackers.

There were walks of bread-crusts leading from house to house and forming streets, and the place seemed to have many inhabitants.

When Dorothy, followed by Billina and Toto, entered the place, they found people walking the streets or assembled in groups talking together, or sitting upon the porches and balconies.

And what funny people they were!

Men, women and children were all made of buns and bread. Some were thin and others fat; some were white, some light brown and some very dark of complexion. A few of the buns, which seemed to form the more important class of the people, were neatly frosted. Some had raisins for eyes and currant buttons on their clothes; others had eyes of cloves and legs of stick cinnamon, and many wore hats and bonnets frosted pink and green.

L. Frank Baum
The Emerald City of Oz

"For an hour past." the Pastor went on, "Mrs. Grant has been sitting with the General. When she speaks to him he opens his eyes. She says little and bears up wonderfully. As he is going, there is a change apparent in everything except his head. The broad forehead is as fine and commanding as ever. The head has not been seen to advantage in his sick chair, but now that he is recumbent it stands boldly out in the wreck of body. It has reminded me over and over again tonight of the death mask of Peter the Great."

While Mrs. Grant sat by the General the other members of the family kept either in the other parts of the room or on the porch, almost within whispering call. They did not care to risk annoyance to him by grouping about him before it became necessary.

The rays of the morning sun fell across the cottage porch upon a family waiting only for death.

The New York Times
July 24, 1885

38

Rosanna found him again after luncheon shaking his little foot from the depths of the piazza chair, but now on their own scene and at a point where this particular feature of it, the cool spreading verandah, commanded the low green cliff and a part of the immediate approach to the house from the seaward side.

Henry James
The Ivory Tower

A small wooden house dominated the camp ground, and on the porch of the house a petrol lantern hissed and threw its white glare in a great circle. Half a dozen tents were pitched near the house, and cars stood beside the tents. Cooking for the night was over, but the coals of the camp-fires still glowed on the ground by the camping places. A group of men had gathered to the porch where the lantern burned, and their faces were strong and muscled under the harsh white light, light that threw black shadows of their hats over their foreheads and eyes and made their chins seem to jut out. They sat on the steps, and some stood on the ground, resting their elbows on the porch floor. The proprietor, a sullen lanky man, sat in a chair on the porch. He leaned back against the wall, and he drummed his fingers on his knee. Inside the house a kerosene lamp burned, but its thin light was blasted by the hissing glare of the petrol lantern. The gathering of men surrounded the proprietor.

John Steinbeck
The Grapes of Wrath

President Truman has left the neo-Roman slabs of Washington to go home to Independence in Missouri, where he can feel more comfortable sitting on the back porch of an old frame house.

Manchester Guardian Weekly
December 30, 1948

45

"Hey, Lord!" STAMP. "Hey, Lord!" STAMP. "Don't wanna ride on the devil's side...just wanna ride with You!"

Zoo squeezed the music from a toy-like accordion, and pounded her flat foot on the rickety cabin-porch floor. "Oh devil done weep, devil done cried, cause he gonna miss me on my last lonesome ride." A prolonged shout: a fillet of gold glistened in the frightening volcano of her mouth, and the little mail-order accordion, shoved in, shoved out, was like a lung of pleated paper and pearl shell. "Gonna miss me..."

For some time the rainbird had shrilled its cool promise from an elderberry lair, and the sun was locked in a tomb of clouds, tropical clouds that nosed across the low sky, massing into a mammoth grey mountain.

Jesus Fever sat surrounded by a mound of beautiful scrap-quilt pillows in a rocker fashioned out of old barrel-staves; his reverent falsetto quavered like a broken ocarina-note, and occasionally he raised his hands to give a feeble, soundless clap.

"...on my ride!"

Truman Capote
Other Voices, Other Rooms

I lie awake a long time, for the night is too rare to be wasted in mere slumber, and listen to the country noises, the baying of the hounds, the chirping of crickets, the far-off eerie call of a screech-owl, the booming of the bullfrogs in the lake. There is an exquisite transition state between consciousness and slumber that I am never aware of in inside sleeping. I sleep at once more deeply and more consciously in the open than within stuffy houses.

Dorothy Scarborough
From A Southern Porch

Then the old man he signed a pledge—made his mark. The judge said it was the holiest time on record, or something like that. Then they tucked the old man into a beautiful room, which was the spare room, and in the night sometime he got powerful thirsty and clumb out onto the porch-roof and slid down a stanchion and traded his new coat for a jug of forty-rod, and clumb back again and had a good old time; and towards daylight he crawled out again, drunk as a fiddler, and rolled off the porch and broke his left arm in two places, and was most froze to death when somebody found him after sun-up. And when they come to look at that spare room, they had to take soundings before they could navigate it.

The judge he felt kind of sore. He said he reckoned a body could reform the ole man with a shotgun, maybe, but he didn't know no other way.

Mark Twain
Adventures of Huckleberry Finn

51

We meet on democracy's front porch, a good place to talk as friends. For this is a day when our nation is made whole, when our differences, for a moment, are suspended.

President George Bush
Inaugural Address, 1989

The girls get at the piano immediately after breakfast; and Ned and myself usually commence the morning with a stroll. If there happen to be visitors to Swallow Barn, this after-breakfast hour is famous for debates. We then all assemble in the porch, and fall into grave discussions upon agriculture, hunting, or horsemanship, in neither of which do I profess any great proficiency, though I take care not to allow that to appear.

John Pendleton Kennedy
Swallow Barn: A Sojourn in the Old Dominion

She began to enjoy sitting on the porch with him, but she could never tell if he knew she was there or not. Even when he answered her, she couldn't tell if he knew it was she. She herself. Mrs. Flood, the landlady. Not just anybody. They would sit, he only sit, and she sit rocking, for half an afternoon and not two words seemed to pass between them, though she might talk at length.

Flannery O'Connor
Wise Blood

S omewhere in the darkness a clock strikes two
   And there is no sound in the sad old house
But the long veranda dripping with dew
And in the wainscot a mouse.

Bret Harte
From "A Newport Romance"

A porch strengthens or conveys expression of purpose, because, instead of leaving the entrance door bare, as in manufactories and buildings of an inferior description, it serves both as a note of preparation, and an effectual shelter and protection to the entrance. Besides this, it gives a dignity and importance to that entrance, pointing it out to the stranger as the place of approach. A fine country house, without a porch or covered shelter to the doorway of some description, is therefore, as incomplete, to the correct eye, as a well-printed book without a title page, leaving the stranger to plunge at once in *media res*, without the friendly preparation of a single word of introduction. Porches are susceptible of every variety of form and decoration, from the embattled and buttressed portal of the Gothic castle, to the latticed arbor-porch of the cottage, around which the festoons of luxuriant climbing plants cluster, giving an effect not less beautiful than the richly carved capitals of the classic portico.

Andrew Jackson Downing
Landscape Architecture

The men worked peacefully and evenly in the shoe-shops all day; and the women stayed at home and kept the little white cottages tidy, cooked the meals, and washed the clothes, and did the sewing. For recreation the men sat on the piazza in front of Barker's store of an evening, and gossiped or discussed politics; and the women talked over their neighbors' fences, or took their sewing into their neighbors' of an afternoon.

Mary E. Wilkins
Two Old Lovers

In the South, when a person plans a home, he first builds a porch, and then if he has any money left, he adds few or more rooms according to his needs, but the porch is the essential thing. One college professor that I know, who had only a limited sum with which to build a home, insisted that he must have at least a bathroom in addition to his veranda, all other quarters being, if necessary, dispensable. But the rise in contractors' prices, with no corresponding elevation of professorial salaries, had reduced him to the necessity of relinquishing either the one or the other. Since he could not have a bathroom and a porch, he said he would put his bathtub on his porch. Even so, he would have a home, for while in New York every man's house is his prison, in the South every man's porch is his home.

Dorothy Scarborough
From A Southern Porch

The maples bending o'er the gate,
   Their arch of leaves just tinted
With yellow warmth, the golden glow
Of coming autumn hinted.

Keen white between the farm-house shared,
And smiled on porch and trellis,
The fair democracy of flowers
That equals cot and palace.

John Greenleaf Whittier
"Among the Hills"

The people all saw her come because it was sundown. The sun was gone, but he had left his footprints in the sky. It was the time for sitting on porches beside the road. It was the time to hear things and talk. These sitters had been tongueless, earless, eyeless conveniences all day long. Mules and other brutes had occupied their skins. But now, the sun and the bossman were gone, so the skins felt powerful and human. They became lords of sounds and lesser things. They passed nations through their mouths. They sat in judgment.

Zora Neale Hurston
Their Eyes Were Watching God

"I must look up a civilized house to lodge in." thought the stranger. "I cannot possibly camp at the tavern. Its offence is rum. and it smells to heaven."

Presently our explorer found a neat. white. two-story. home-like abode on the upper street. overlooking the river.

"This promises." he thought. "Here are roses on the porch. a piano. or at least a melodeon. by the parlor-window. and they are insured in the Mutual. as the Mutual's plate announces. Now. if that nice-looking person in black I see setting a table in the back-room is a widow. I will camp here."

Theodore Winthrop
Life in the Open Air

You say you don't know what I mean by peaza. I will tell you than. It is exactly such a thing as the cover over the pump in your Yard, suppose no enclosure for Poultry their, and 3 or 4 posts added to support the front of the Roof, a good floor at bottum, and from post to post a Chinese enclosure about three feet high. These posts are Scantlings of 6 to 4 inches Diameter, the Broad side to the front, with only a little moulding round the top in a neat plain manner. Some have collums but very few, and the top is generally plastered, but I think if the top was sealed with neat plain Boards I should like it as well. These Peazas are so cool in Sumer and in Winter break off the storms so much that I think I should not be able to like an house without….

John Singleton Copley
Letter to Henry Pelham, July 14, 1771

L ater in the day, the ladies were gathered in the end piazza, while some of the older ones played croquet on the lawn...there were settees, and regular piazza chairs,—stiff enough, of plain deal, with no cushions, and there were one or two comfortable low Shaker chairs, and a couple of stuffed rockers. Mrs Regis, of course, was established in one of the last, and all the rest were occupied.

"I wonder why they make uncomfortable chairs at all!" said Mrs Regis. "If I had the ordering there shouldn't be anything manufactured that wasn't low and broad and easy."

Adeline Dutton Train Whitney
Sights and Insights, Volume 1

In my childhood, the porch was a concept as well as a place. In Mobile, Alabama, everybody would always sit on the front porch shelling peas and exchanging the neighborhood gossip. If my grandmother sat facing the street, that meant she would "receive": other ladies, across the street, next door, or passing by, could come up on the porch and talk to her.

If she sat sidewise, with her profile to the street, you could greet her and speak to her from the sidewalk but you couldn't come up onto the porch. If she sat with her back to the street, she was invisible. It meant that she was reading the paper or hadn't done her hair yet. You wouldn't say anything to her.

Eugene Walter
"Secrets of a Southern Porch," The New Yorker, June 1998

Part of the broad significance of my grandmother's front porch came through the stories my mother told. Before she passed away in 1997, my mother, Marie Foreman Hazelwood, frequently recalled porch memories of family and community. She talked of how she and her family would, on hot summer evenings, burn old rags to keep the mosquitoes away while catching up on stories. She recalled how she and my dad courted on the front porch swing. She even talked of the porch's political significance in the following story about the election returns of 1932, the year Franklin Delano Roosevelt was first voted into office: "One of my earliest memories—when I was about four or five—was when I first heard the presidential election returns broadcast over the radio. We were one of the few families in Moss Bluff who had a radio, so Daddy moved it out on the porch so that a lot of our relatives—Aunt Della, Uncle Mip, Aunt Cecile—and a lot of people from the community could come over to hear the returns. There must have been about fifty people there, standing on the porch, where the radio was set up on a long table. When Roosevelt won, they played the song "Happy Days Are Here Again," and it was the first time I ever heard that song. Every time I hear it I think about that night that Daddy moved the radio out on the porch…."

Jocelyn Hazelwood Donlon
Swinging in Place: Porch Life in Southern Culture

I t's the mugginess that gets you. Step outside in Iowa in August and within 20 seconds you will experience a condition that might be called perspiration incontinence. It gets so hot that you will see department store mannequins with sweat circles under their arms. I have particularly vivid memories of Iowa summers because my father was the last person in the Midwest to buy an air-conditioner. He thought they were unnatural. (He thought anything that cost more than $30 was unnatural.)

The one place you could get a little relief was the screened porch. Up until the 1950s nearly every American home had one of these. A screened porch is a kind of summer room on the side of the house, with walls made of a fine but sturdy mesh to keep out insects. They give you all the advantages of being outdoors and indoors at the same time. They are wonderful and will always be associated in my mind with summer things—corn on the cob, water-melon, the nighttime chirr of crickets....

Bill Bryson
Notes from a Big Country

L eft thus to herself, though conscious she well might have visitors, she circled slowly and repeatedly round the gallery....

Henry James
The Ivory Tower

...**W**e recommend to all Philadelphians, who thirst for the breath of the mountains, and are willing to breathe it within the limits of their own noble State, to repair to the Delaware Water-Gap, sit them down in the porch of our friend Snyder, discourse with him concerning trout, deer and rattlesnakes, and make themselves at home with him for a week.

Robert Montgomery Bird
The Hawks of Hawk Hollow

When I removed into the country, it was to occupy an old-fashioned farmhouse, which had no piazza—a deficiency the more regretted because not only did I like piazzas, as somehow combining the coziness of indoors with the freedom of out-doors, and it is so pleasant to inspect your thermometer there, but the country round about was such a picture that in berry time no boy climbs hill or crosses vale without coming upon easels planted in every nook, and sunburnt painters painting there. A very paradise of painters. The circle of the stars cut by the circle of the mountains. At least, so looks it from the house; though, once upon the mountains, no circle of them can you see. Had the site been chosen five rods off, this charmed ring would not have been.

Herman Melville
The Piazza

She sits in an arm-chair, under
the shaded porch of the farm-house,
The sun just shines on her old white head.

Walt Whitman
From "Faces"

They swarmed up in front of Sherburn's palings as thick as they could jam together, and you couldn't hear yourself think for the noise. It was a little twenty-foot yard. Some sung out "Tear down the fence! tear down the fence!" Then there was a racket of ripping and tearing and smashing, and down she goes, and the front wall of the crowd begins to roll in like a wave.

Just then Sherburn steps out on to the roof of his little front porch, with a double-barrel gun in his hand, and takes his stand, perfectly ca'm and deliberate, not saying a word. The racket stopped, and the wave sucked back.

Mark Twain
Adventures of Huckleberry Finn

... **T**he piazza politician, sipping his toddy, spreading his legs, and discussing constitutional issues on the spacious verandahs of open-air Virginia...felt the stress of the time and thrilled unequivocally with the sensation of foreshadowing change.

James Albert Harrison
George Washington: Patriot, Soldier, Statesman,
First President of the United States

The soft sunset of April, of an April sky in Carolina, lay beautifully over the scene that afternoon. Imbowered in trees, with a gentle esplanade, running down to the river, stood the pretty yet modest cottage....The dwelling was prettily enclosed with sheltering groves—through which, at spots here and there, peered forth its well whitewashed veranda....The house itself was rude enough—like those of the region generally, having been built of logs....We should not forget to insist upon the porch or portico of four columns, formed of slender pines decapitated for the purpose, which, having its distinct roof, formed the entrance through the piazza to the humble cottage....

William Gilmore Simms
The Yemassee

I t is time now for the small town people to be out of doors. In most of the countries of an old European world the summer life of the people in the towns is led in gardens back of the houses but here, in North America, we live during the hot months at the front of the house. We live on the front porch.

The people of the towns sit in groups on their front porches. In the warm darkness, on summer evenings, there is a movement from house to house, visits made back and forth, low-voiced talk going on.

Sherwood Anderson
Home Town

Mr. Pontellier finally lit a cigar and began to smoke, letting the paper drag idly from his hand. He fixed his gaze upon a white sunshade that was advancing at snail's pace from the beach. He could see it plainly between the gaunt trunks of the water oaks and across the stretch of yellow camomile. The gulf looked far away, melting hazily into the blue of the horizon. The sunshade continued to approach slowly. Beneath its pink-lined shelter were his wife, Mrs. Pontellier, and young Robert Lebrun. When they reached the cottage, the two seated themselves with some appearance of fatigue upon the upper step of the porch, facing each other, each leaning against a supporting post.

"What folly! to bathe at such an hour in such heat!" exclaimed Mr. Pontellier.

Kate Chopin
The Awakening

T hose horses coming into the stretch at Ruidoso!
    Mist rising from the meadow at dawn.
From the veranda, the blue outlines of the mountains.
What used to be within reach, out of reach.
And in some lesser things, just the opposite is true.

Raymond Carver
From "The Garden"

This brother I say, quarrelled with me, though I had borne from him unresentingly, what from another would have seemed insult. We quarrelled at last, and the house was closed to me, or would have been had I sought access: for I walked sternly past its pleasant door that afternoon, though I remember now how the very roses that o'erhung the porch, the benched and shaded porch, that lovely lingering place, seemed to beckon me in. It was a breathless summer day, and the vine curled in the open window,—even now those lowly rooms make a brighter image of heaven to me than the jewelled walls that of old grew in the pageant of our sabbath dreams.

Delia Salter Bacon
The Bride of Fort Edward

The distant point of the ridge, like the tongue of a calf, put its red lick on the sky. Mists, voids, patches of woods and naked clay, flickered like live ashes, pink and blue. A mirror that hung within the porch on the house wall began to flicker as at the striking of kitchen matches. Suddenly two chinaberry trees at the foot of the yard lit up, like roosters astrut with golden tails. Caterpillar nets shone in the pecan tree. A swollen shadow bulked underneath it, familiar in shape as Noah's Ark—a school bus.

Then as if something came sliding out of the sky, the whole tin roof of the house ran with new blue. The posts along the porch softly bloomed downward, as if chalk marks were being drawn, one more time, down a still misty slate. The house was revealed as if standing there from pure memory against a now moonless sky. For the length of a breath, everything stayed shadowless, as under a lifting hand, and then a passage showed, running through the house, right through the middle of it, and at the head of the passage, in the center of the front gallery, a figure was revealed, a very old lady seated in a rocking chair with head cocked, as though wild to be seen.

Eudora Welty
Losing Battles

A country house without a porch is like a man without an eyebrow.

D. G. Mitchell
Rural Studies with Hints for Country Places

Index of Authors

Acknowledgments

Note: Every effort has been made to contact current copyright holders. Any omission is unintentional, and the publisher would be pleased to hear from any copyright holders not acknowledged below.

p.9 From *Veranda: Embracing Place* by Philip Drew. Copyright © 1992 by Philip Drew. By permission of HarperCollins Publishers. **p.13** From *Gone With the Wind* by Margaret Mitchell. Copyright © 1936 by Macmillan Publishing Company, a division of Macmillan, Inc. Copyright renewed © 1964 by Stephens Mitchell and Trust Company of Georgia as Executors of Margaret Mitchell Marsh. By permission of William Morris Agency, Inc. on behalf of the Author. **p.14** From *A Death in the Family* by James Agee, copyright © 1957 by The James Agee Trust, renewed 1985 by Mia Agee. By permission of Grosset & Dunlap, Inc., a division of Penguin Putnam Inc. **p.17** From *Fahrenheit 451* by Ray Bradbury (HarperCollins, 1953). By permission of Don Congdon Associates Inc., copyright © 1953, renewed 1981 by Ray Bradbury. **p.20** From *To Kill a Mockingbird* by Harper Lee published by Heinemann. Copyright © Harper Lee, 1960. By permission of The Random House Group Ltd. and Gillon Aitken Associates Ltd. **p.23** From *Look Homeward, Angel* by Thomas Wolfe. By permission of Scribner, an imprint of Simon and Schuster Adult Publishing Group and Eugene Winick, Administrator C.T.A. of the Estate of Thomas Wolfe. Copyright © 1929 by Charles Scribner's Sons and by Thomas Wolfe; copyright renewed © 1957 by Edward C. Ashwell, Administrator, C.T.A. and/or Fred W. Wolfe. **p.26** From *The Great Gatsby* by F. Scott Fitzgerald (Penguin Books, 1994). By permission of David Higham Associates, and Scribner, an imprint of Simon & Schuster Adult Publishing Group. Copyright © 1925 by Charles Scribner's Sons. Copyright renewed 1953 by Frances Scott Fitzgerald Lanahan. **p.35** From *Divine Secrets of the Ya-Ya Sisterhood* by Rebecca Wells. Copyright © 1996 by Rebecca Wells. By permission of Macmillan, London, UK. **p.46** From *Other Voices, Other Rooms* by Truman Capote published by William Heinemann. By permission of The Random House Group Ltd. Copyright © 1948 by Truman Capote. **p.56** Excerpt from *Wise Blood* by Flannery O'Connor. Copyright © 1962 by Flannery O'Connor. Copyright renewed © 1990 by Regina O'Connor. Reprinted by permission of Farrar, Straus and Giroux, LLC. **p.68** From *Their Eyes Were Watching God* by Zora Neale Hurston. By permission of the Estate of Zora Neale Hurston. **p.79** From *Swinging in Place: Porch Life in Southern Culture* by Jocelyn Hazelwood Donlon. Copyright © 2001 by The University of North Carolina Press. By permission of the publisher. **p.96** From *Home Town* by Sherwood Anderson. Copyright © 1940 by Sherwood Anderson. By permission of Harold Ober Associates Incorporated. **p.100** Extract from "The Garden" from *All of Us* by Raymond Carver published by The Harvill Press © Tess Gallagher. By permission of The Random House Group Limited and International Creative Management, Inc. **p.105** From *Losing Battles* by Eudora Welty (Virago Press Ltd., 1982). By permission of Time Warner Books UK.

Photo Credits

Cover image © Phil Schermeister/CORBIS; **p.2/88** © William A. Bake/CORBIS; **p.5/41** © Kelly-Mooney Photography/CORBIS; **p.6** © Philip Gould/CORBIS; **p.8** © Kelly-Mooney Photography/CORBIS; **p.11** © James L. Amos/CORBIS; **p.12** © Angelo Hornak/CORBIS; **p.15** © Lee Snider; Lee Snider/CORBIS; **p.16** © Franz-Marc Frei/CORBIS; **p.19** © Lee Snider; Lee Snider/CORBIS; **p.21** © Carol Cohen/CORBIS; **p.22** © Craig Lovell/CORBIS; **p.24** © Kevin Fleming/CORBIS; **p.27** © Bob Krist/CORBIS; **p.28** © Richard Bickel/CORBIS; **p.31** © James Blair/CORBIS; **p.32** © Kit Kittle/CORBIS; **p.34** © Julie Habel/CORBIS; **p.37** © James L. Amos/CORBIS; **p.39** © Morton Beebe; S. F./CORBIS; **p.42** © William A. Bake/CORBIS; **p.44** © Phil Schermeister/CORBIS; **p.47** © Kevin R. Morris/CORBIS; **p.49** © Todd Gipstein/CORBIS; **p.50** © Franz-Marc Frei/CORBIS; **p.52** © Owen Franken/CORBIS; **p.54** © The Purcell Team/CORBIS; **p.57** © Farrell Grehan/CORBIS; **p.58** © Alain Le Garsmeur/CORBIS; **p.61** © Todd Gipstein/CORBIS; **p.63** © David H. Wells/CORBIS; **p.64** © Michael Lewis/CORBIS; **p.67** © William A. Bake/CORBIS; **p.69** © Kevin Fleming/CORBIS; **p.71** © Philippa Lewis; Edifice/CORBIS; **p.72** © Alain Le Garsmeur/CORBIS; **p.74** © Robert Holmes/CORBIS; **p.77** © Franz-Marc Frei/CORBIS; **p.78** © Owen Franken/CORBIS; **p.81** © Philip Gould/CORBIS; **p.83** © Lee Snider; Lee Snider/CORBIS; **p.85** © Peter Beck/CORBIS; **p.86** © Philip Gould/CORBIS; **p.91** © Bettmann/CORBIS; **p.92** © Lee Snider; Lee Snider/CORBIS; **p.94** © Philip Gould/CORBIS; **p.102** © Philippa Lewis; Edifice/CORBIS; **p.98** © Richard Bickel/CORBIS; **p.101** © William A. Bake/CORBIS; **p.102** © Philippa Lewis; Edifice/CORBIS; **p.104** © James L. Amos/CORBIS; **p.107** © Kevin Fleming/CORBIS

First edition for North America published in 2003
by Barron's Educational Series, Inc.

All rights reserved. No part of this book may be reproduced
in any form, by photostat, microfilm, xerography, or any
other means, or incorporated into any information retrieval
system, electronic or mechanical, without the written
permission of the copyright owner.

Copyright © 2003 MQ Publications Ltd

MQ Publications Ltd
12 The Ivories
6-8 Northampton Street
London N1 2HY
United Kingdom

Anthologist: Wynn Wheldon
Design: Philippa Jarvis
Editor: Leanne Bryan

All inquiries should be addressed to:
Barron's Educational Series, Inc.
250 Wireless Boulevard
Hauppauge, NY 11788
http://www.barronseduc.com

Library of Congress Catalog Card No.: 2002111570

International Standard Book No.: 0-7641-5582-2

Printed in China
9 8 7 6 5 4 3 2 1